MYSTERIES TO EXPLORE

ROAR!

The Story of ROANOKE

by Noah Leatherland

BEARPORT PUBLISHING

Roar! Books, an imprint of Bearport Publishing by FlutterBee

Credits
Cover and title page, © Zack Frank/Adobe Stock and © Library of Congress/Geography and Map Division; 4–5, © stevemart/Shutterstock; 5, © patpitchaya/Shutterstock; 6, © Ivy Close Images/Alamy Stock Photo; 7M, © pingebat/Shutterstock; 7BR, © Lisa/Adobe Stock; 8, © Universal History Archive/Getty Images; 8–9, © 1000 Words/Shutterstock; 9, © pingebat/Shutterstock; 10, © Irina Gutyryak/Shutterstock; 11, © Zack Frank/Shutterstock; 12–13, © DEA / G. DAGLI ORTI/Getty Images; 13, © North Wind Picture Archives/Alamy Stock Photo; 14MR, © William James Linton/Wikimedia; 14–15, © Zack Frank/Shutterstock; 15TR, © Public Domain/Wikimedia; 16–17, © Public Domain/Wikimedia; 17, © Fredlyfish4/Shutterstock; 18–19, © Stock Montage/Getty Images; 19, © Library of Congress/Geography and Map Division; 20, © Godfrey Kneller/Wikimedia; 21TL, © Public Domain/Wikimedia; 21M, © msc56/iStock; 22–23, © Wendy/Wikimedia; 23M, © AP Photo; 23BR, © Nesnad/Wikimedia; 24, © /; 25, © Wicked Digital/Shutterstock; 26–27, © William Silver/Shutterstock; 27, © Carol M. Highsmith Archive./Library of Congress; 28–29, © Zack Frank/Shutterstock; 29, © AP Photo; 30, © NayaDadara/Shutterstock; 31, © M. Timothy O'Keefe/Alamy Stock Photo

Bearport Publishing Company Product Development Team
Kayla Eggert, Theresa Emminizer, Kim Jones, Allison Juda, Cole Nelson, Naomi Reich, Steve Scheluchin, Tiana Tran

Library of Congress Cataloging-in-Publication Data is available at www.loc.gov or upon request from the publisher.

ISBN: 979-8-89577-842-5 (hardcover)
ISBN: 979-8-89577-850-0 (ebook)

For more information, write to Bearport Publishing, 3500 American Blvd W, Suite 150, Bloomington, MN 55431. Printed in the United States of America.

CONTENTS

HISTORY'S MYSTERIES

Most stories have a beginning and an end. However, some of them leave behind more questions than answers.

These tales have missing information or unlikely endings.

People have tried to solve famous mysteries for many years. Despite their efforts, parts of some of these stories remain unexplained.

Are you ready to explore a mystery?

THE MYSTERY OF THE LOST COLONY

The disappearance of the members of the Roanoke Colony is one of the most famous mysteries in history. The colony is often referred to as the Lost Colony.

A colony is a piece of land in a foreign place that a country claims for their people to live there. In the late 16th century, countries sent people far and wide to set up colonies.

Because colonies were usually far away, getting news from them often took a long time.

No one would know if something bad occured. This long wait adds to the mystery of what happened on Roanoke Island.

BEFORE THE MYSTERY

Queen Elizabeth I wanted to set up a colony in North America. She hoped this would give the British Empire power against Spain.

Sir Walter Raleigh was put in charge of setting up this colony. He sent two explorers, Philip Amadas and Arthur Barlowe, to find a place for settlement.

In 1584, the two explorers came across Roanoke Island. However, the island was not deserted.

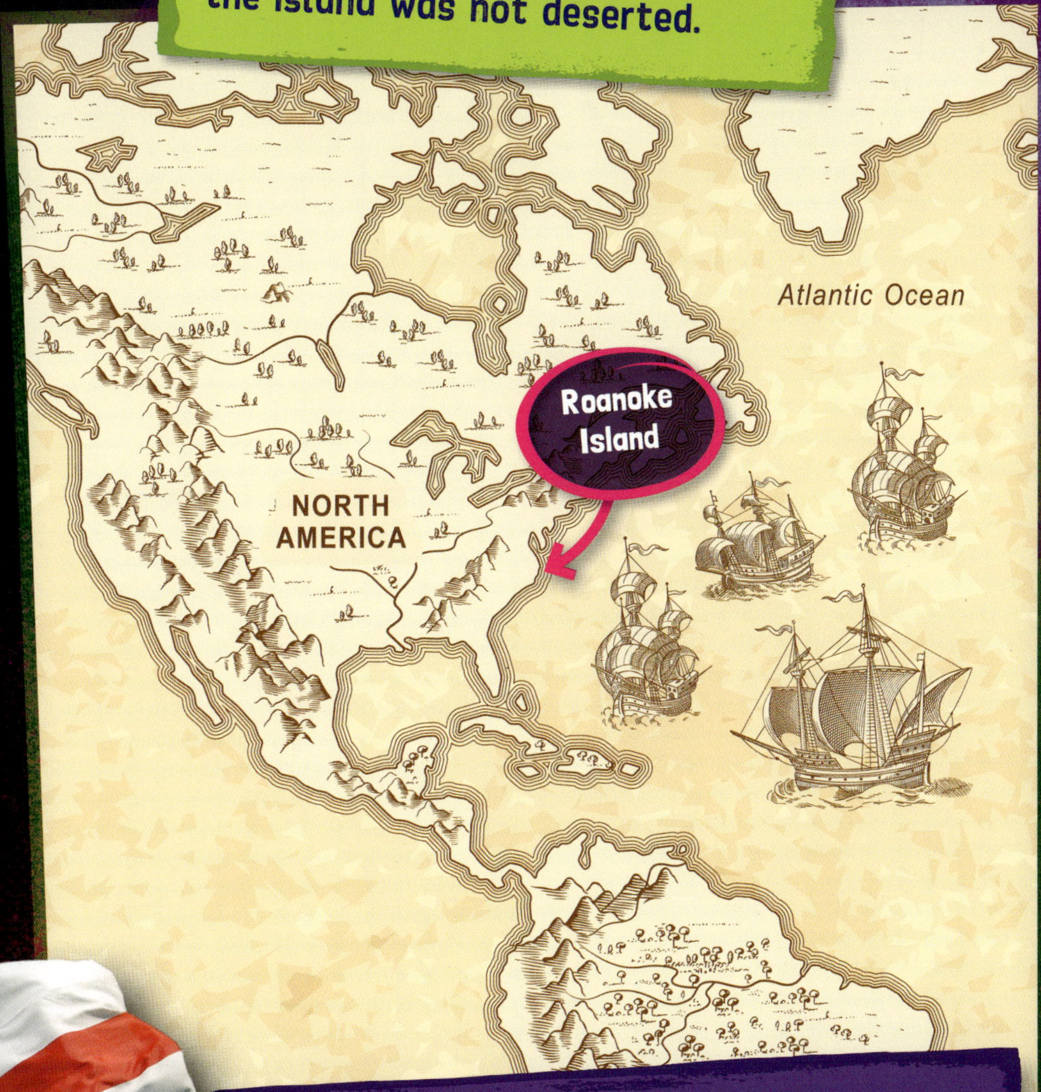

Indigenous people already lived there. Amadas and Barlowe made friendly contact with them before returning to England and reporting their findings.

ROANOKE ISLAND

Amadas and Barlowe thought Roanoke would be the perfect place for a colony.

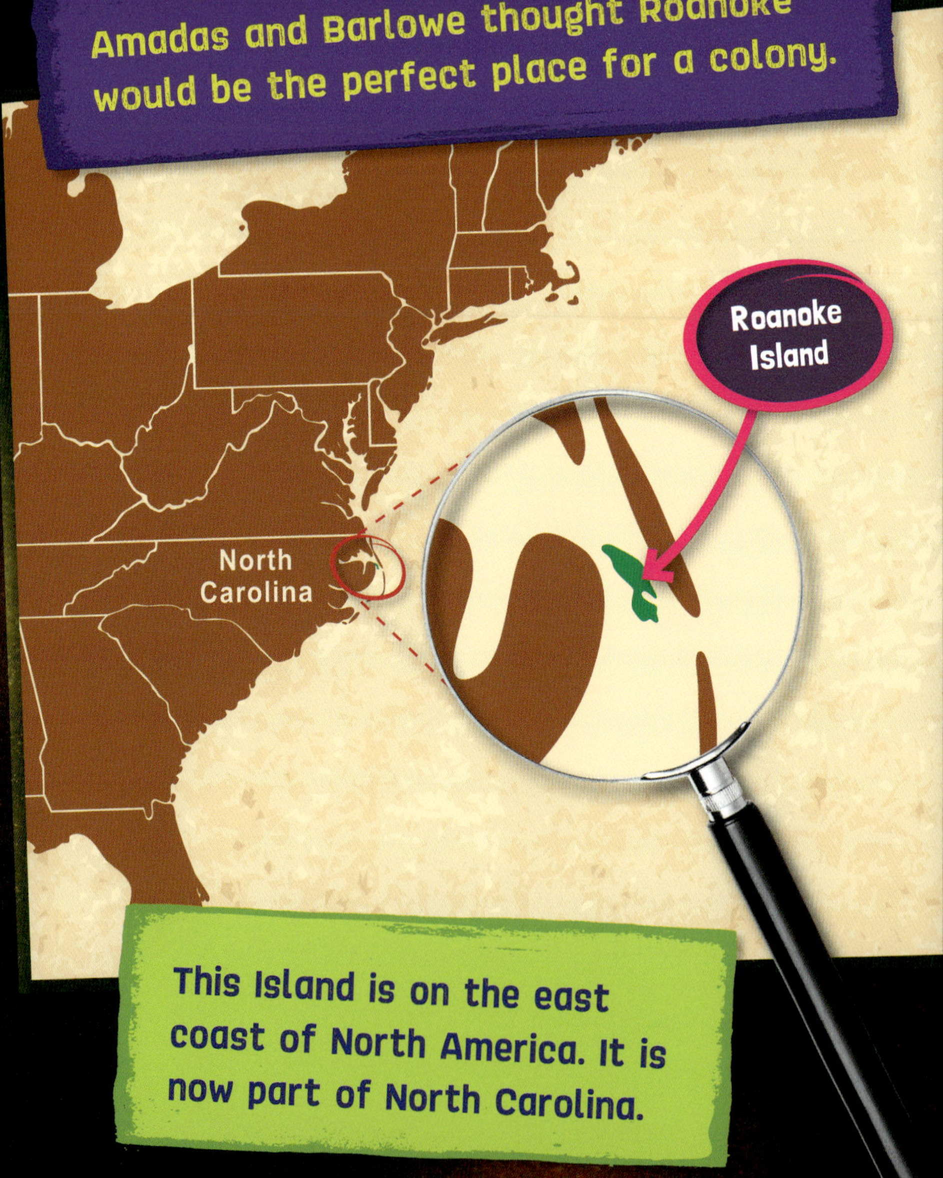

This Island is on the east coast of North America. It is now part of North Carolina.

This small island is between the mainland of North Carolina and barrier islands called the Outer Banks.

The island has good soil for growing plants and plenty of fresh water. These natural resources make it a good place to live.

THE FIRST COLONY

English colonists first set out to make a colony on Roanoke Island in 1585. The colonists brought about 600 people on 7 ships.

Along the way, one of the ships was heavily damaged in a bad storm. Most of its food supplies were destroyed.

Due to lack of food, only 100 colonists stayed on Roanoke Island. The Indigenous peoples on the island helped the newcomers. They shared their resources. However, the colonists took more than their share.

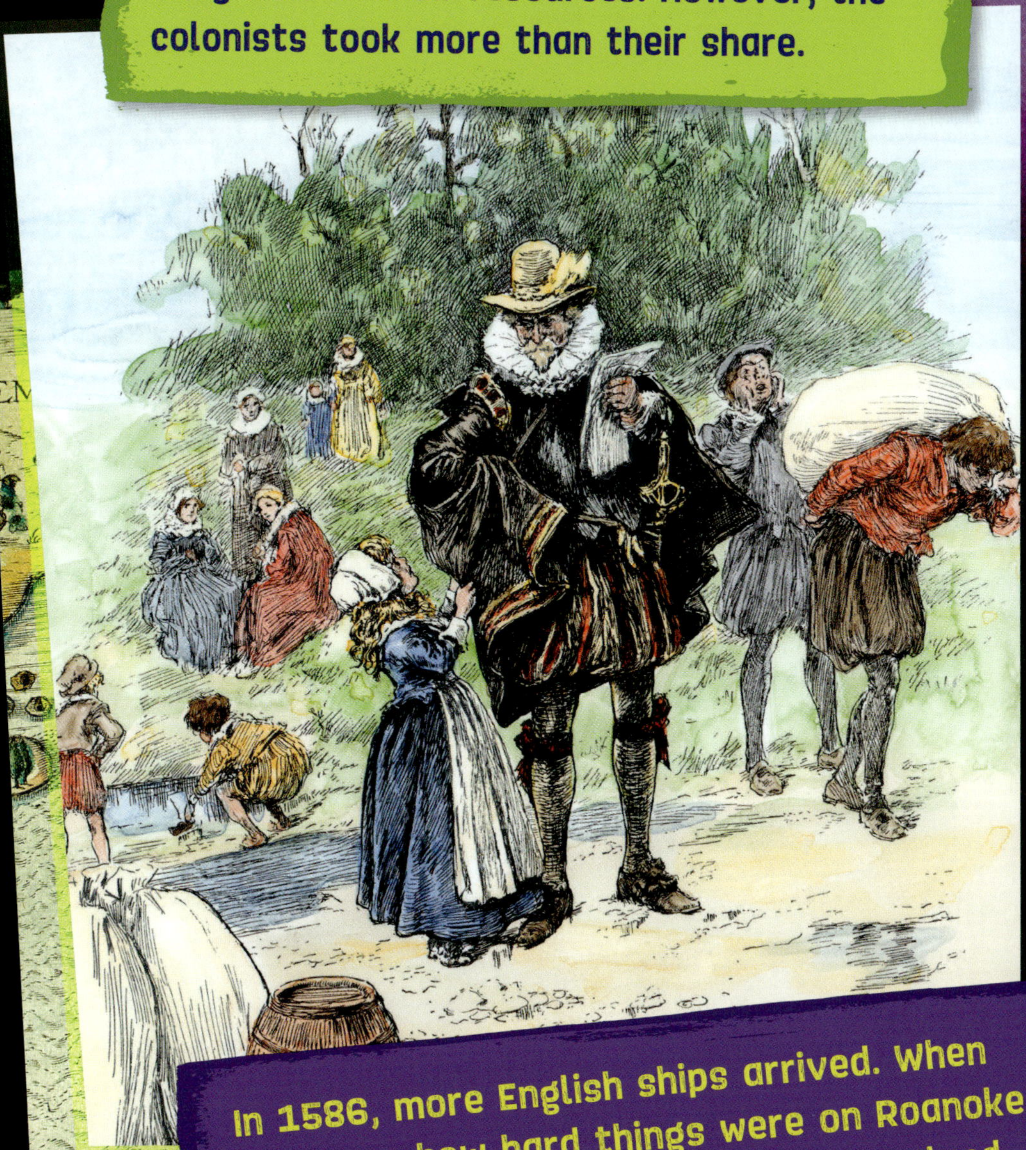

In 1586, more English ships arrived. When they saw how hard things were on Roanoke, most of the people went back to England.

THE SECOND COLONY

The English tried to make a colony on Roanoke Island again in 1587. This time, the group was led by John White.

John White

White took around 100 colonists to the island. The group included his wife, Thomasine, and his daughter, Eleanor Dare.

They landed on Roanoke Island on July 22, 1587. The English built the new colony in the same place as the first one. They even used some of the old buildings.

To prepare for winter, White returned to England. He planned to go home to gather more people and supplies.

STRANGE FINDINGS

White made it back to England on November 8, 1587. But his plans to return to Roanoke had to wait. England was at war with Spain, and they needed all their ships and supplies for the battles.

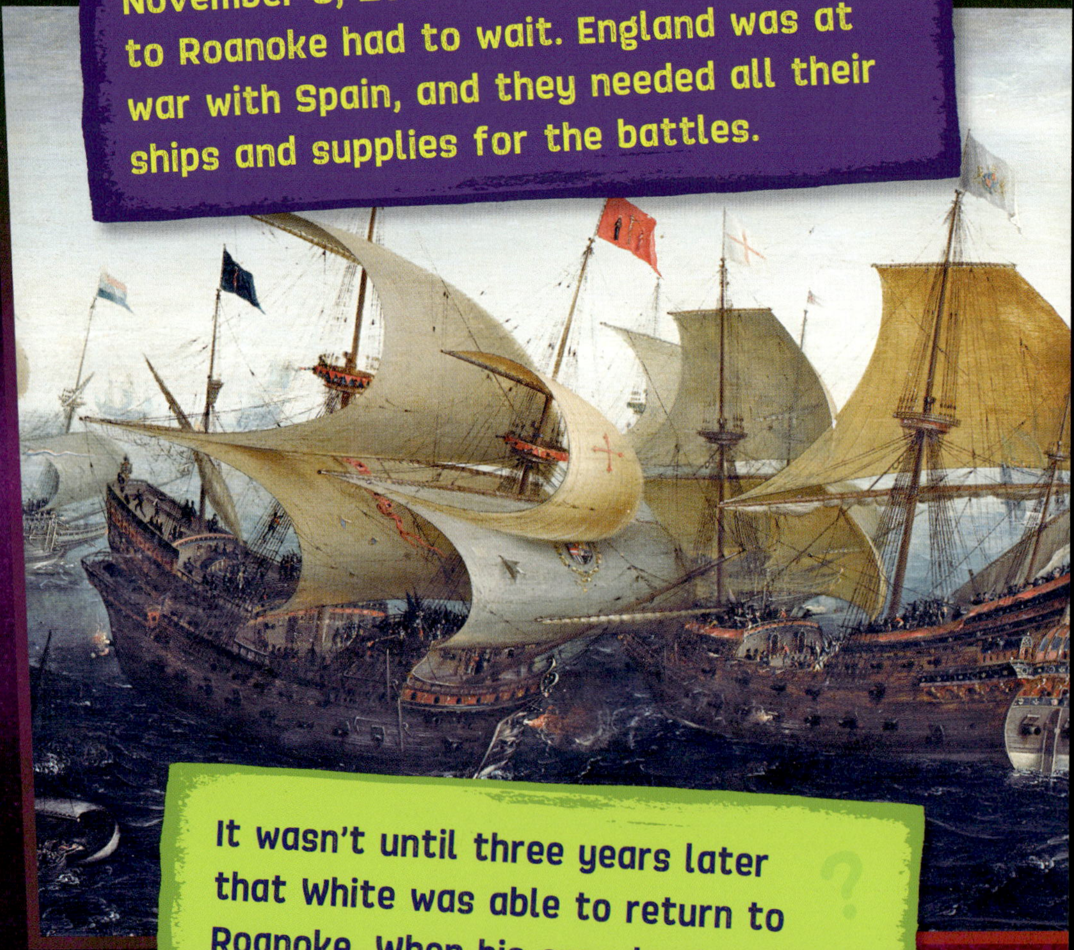

It wasn't until three years later that White was able to return to Roanoke. When his crew landed, they saw smoke coming from the colony.

White and his crew rushed toward the smoke. But when they arrived, they found something strange. . . .

All of the people, including White's family, had disappeared! Their homes were gone, too. Yet, there was no sign of a struggle.

SECRET MESSAGES

Before he left, White had told the colonists to leave him a message if they went anywhere. If they were in danger, they should carve a cross on a tree or a post.

White and his crew found two carvings. One said CRO and the other said CROATOAN. Neither message had a cross.

Croatoan was an island that was not far from Roanoke Island. But a strong hurricane kept White and his crew from sailing there.

White was forced to go back to England. He never saw his family again.

THE HATTERAS TRIBE

It took more than 100 years for new clues about the Lost Colony to turn up.

Explorer John Lawson traveled near Roanoke Island in 1701. He wrote about his journey in a journal.

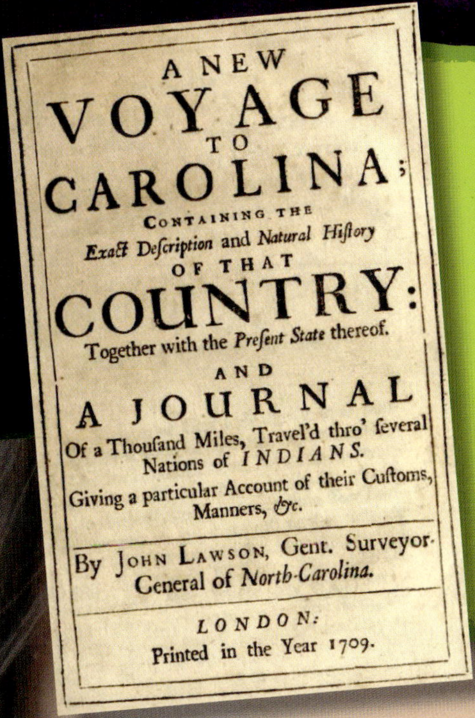

A NEW
VOYAGE
TO
CAROLINA;
CONTAINING THE
Exact Description and *Natural History*
OF THAT
COUNTRY:
Together with the *Present State* thereof.
AND
A JOURNAL
Of a Thousand Miles, Travel'd thro' several
Nations of *INDIANS*.
Giving a particular Account of their Customs,
Manners, &c.

By JOHN LAWSON, Gent. Surveyor-
General of *North-Carolina*.

LONDON:
Printed in the Year 1709.

Lawson mentioned meeting the Hatteras tribe. Some members of this group shared traits with English people, such as light-colored eyes. This could mean the colonists joined the tribe and the group had kids together.

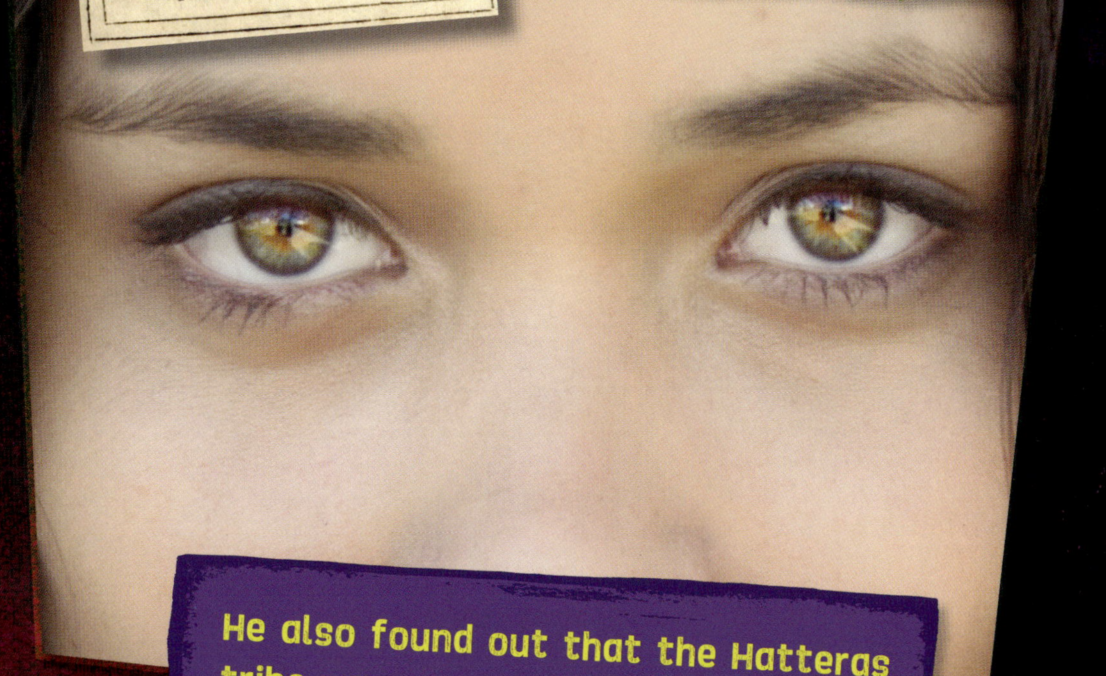

He also found out that the Hatteras tribe were once called the Croatoan tribe. This is the word that White found carved into a post.

THE DARE STONES

In 1937, a strange stone slab was found in a river in North Carolina.

There was writing on the stone. It told the story of how most of the colonists died. It was signed with the initials EWD, which many assumed to be White's daughter. The strange rock came to be called the Dare stone.

Later, more stones were found. But they turned out to be fake. The spelling of some words did not match what would have been used in the 16th century. Additionally, the names of the colonists didn't match known records.

Only the first stone seemed real. Yet, some people think it was still fake.

HIDDEN SYMBOLS

More recently, another hidden clue was uncovered on a map. At the time of the Roanoke colony, maps were painted by hand. Sometimes, patches were stuck on them to cover up mistakes.

In 2012, something strange was found on one of White's watercolor maps. Under a patch, he had a four-pointed star that was colored red and blue.

Researchers believe the star is a hidden symbol for a fort. At the time, people used star symbols to represent locations.

Before White left for England, he told the colonists to move 50 miles (80 km) away. This hidden symbol was placed about that distance from Roanoke Island. However, because of bad weather, White was never able to search this area.

ROANOKE ISLAND TODAY

Today, lots of people live on Roanoke. It is home to more than 6,000 people.

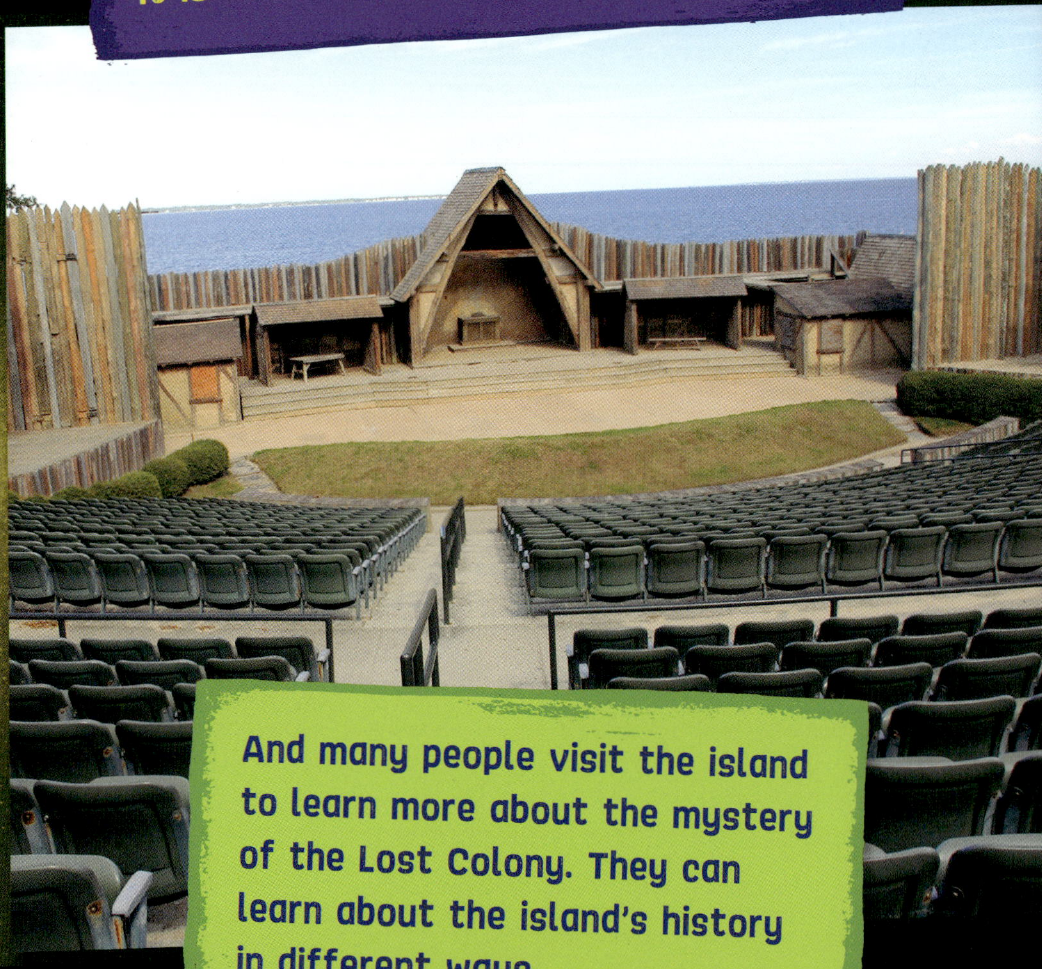

And many people visit the island to learn more about the mystery of the Lost Colony. They can learn about the island's history in different ways.

A local theater group performs the story for tourists. And there is a recreation of the 1585 settlement.

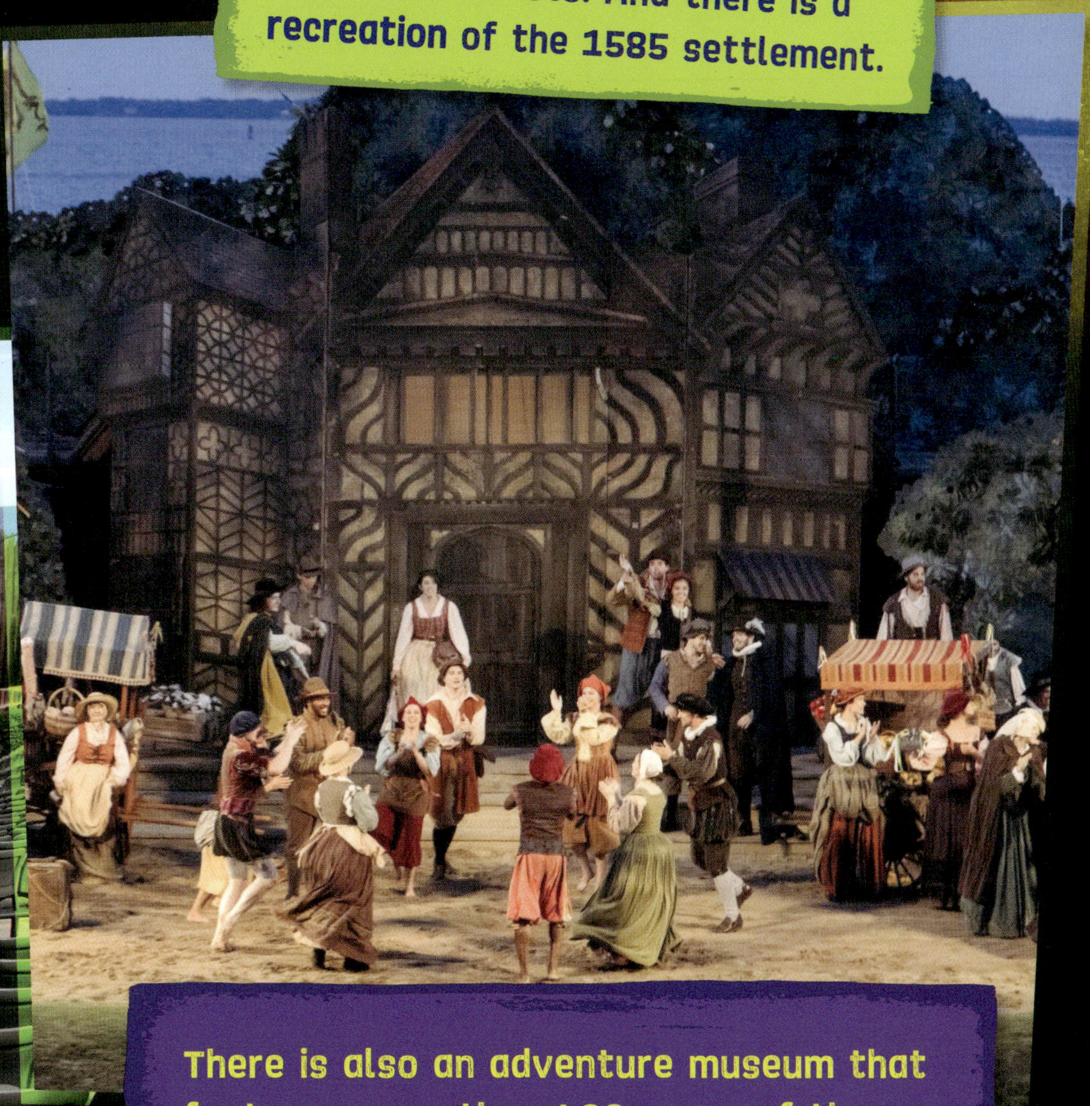

There is also an adventure museum that features more than 400 years of the island's history. Visitors can learn about Indigenous culture, navigation at the time of the old colony, and much more.

FACT OR FICTION?

With so many questions surrounding the Lost Colony, it's hard to tell what is real and what is fake. What are people asking?

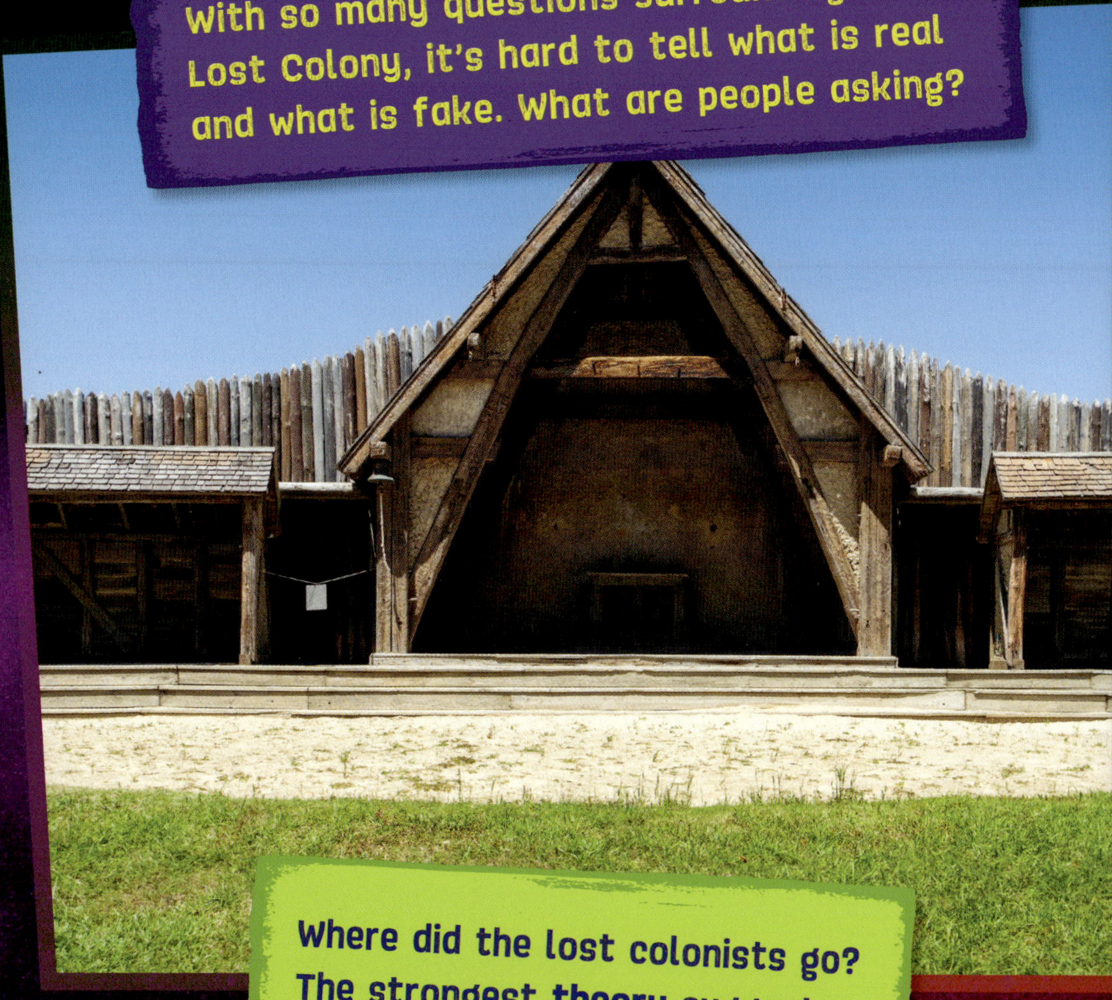

Where did the lost colonists go? The strongest **theory** suggests they went to Croatoan Island.

Were all the Dare stones a hoax? Aside from the first one, the rest of the stones were proven to be fake.

A lot of claims about the Roanoke Colony have never been proven. But the most famous theory is that the colonists joined the Hatteras tribe.

THE TRUTH IS OUT THERE!

There are plenty more clues we might yet uncover to solve the mysteries of the Lost Colony of Roanoke. One day, we might get a step closer to the truth.

It is fun to read about mysteries and wonder about what might have happened. What would you like to explore next?

GLOSSARY

barrier islands long, sandy islands near a shore that stop the worst of severe weather and flooding from reaching the mainland

carvings shapes that have been cut into things

colonists people that go to live in a colony

empires large areas, countries, or regions ruled by a single person

hoax a trick meant to fool people

Indigenous describing the people that originally lived in a certain place

recreation something that was created again

theory an idea used as a possible explanation for something

traits characteristics of a living thing

Index

Read More

Chanez, Katie. *Lost Colony of Roanoke (Mysteries in History).* Minneapolis: Jump!, Inc., 2026.

Kelley, Tera. *Roanoke Colony (Unsolved Mysteries).* Mendota Heights, MN: North Star Editions, 2023.

Sommer, Nathan. *North Carolina (State Profiles).* Minneapolis: Bellwether Media, 2022.

Learn More Online

1. Go to **FactSurfer.com** or scan the QR code below.
2. Enter "**Roanoke Story**" into the search box.
3. Click on the cover of this book to see a list of websites.